Introduction:

MW00916548

This booklet contains a full prac
with the practice experience nee
This practice exam should help you see whether you have not only
memorized your study material, but are also able to apply it, which
is the only way to pass the exam.

There are 90 questions, distributed over 18 cases. The score to aim
for is 80% correct, meaning 18 mistakes or fewer. If you scored
80% or higher, consider yourself ready for exam day.

How to take this practice exam:

Take a piece of paper, a pencil, and a timer. Set the timer for 2.5
hours (although there is more reading during this practice exam
compared to the actual exam). Write down the number of the
question and the answer you think is correct. If you do not
immediately know the correct answer, or you would like to review
your answer at the end, write a question mark behind that question.
This indicates that you flagged the answer for later review, so you
do not waste time if you are stuck (very useful during the actual
exam as well!).

Afterward, go to the answer section of this booklet. The answer
key is provided, which allows you to determine your score. An
explanation is provided in the last section of this booklet. Keep in
mind that it is important to understand the logic behind the
questions and answers, since that is one of the benefits of using
this practice exam.

About this document:

The practice exams currently available are incomplete, expensive, and treacherously easy. This practice exam provides you with more of a challenge than the alternatives. The brief explanations should help you understand the way questions can be phrased and how to choose the best answer.

After using this booklet as intended, combined with your regular study material, you should have improved your speed and accuracy, leaving you with sufficient time to go back to review the questions you flagged.

Good luck!

Kind regards,

Jasper Jacobs, CIPP/E, CIPP/US, CIPM, CIPT

EXAM QUESTIONS:

Midway through your career, you find yourself working for the internal audit department of a large manufacturing company. The company produces mechanical parts, which it ships to Canada, where the parts are assembled into ships. All employee data are shared between the European Union and Canada, because half of the work takes place in the European Union and other half in Canada. This is needed to ensure that all employees are paid and the files of all employees are updated as needed.

The internal audit department performs compliance audits, verifying whether all practices of the company are compliant with legislation and company policy. In the previous years, there have been several severe accidents in organizations with similar activities, therefore a lot of focus is placed on Health & Safety in the manufacturing process. As part of the audit schedule, you perform a Health & Safety audit, since Health & Safety is now high on the company's agenda and the industry is highly regulated.

When you are at the European manufacturing location, you want to check whether all employees have undergone their legally required medical check. This leads to some meddling from the works council. The works council is upset about some of the information that is required for providing assurance that the company complies with the Health & Safety regulations.

1. Which of the following is most likely the case?
A. information on whether a check was performed is sensitive personal data, and consent is needed
B. you are not allowed to perform your check, as it concerns sensitive personal data, and consent cannot be freely given in this scenario
C. you are allowed to check all the documents you want, as you do not need to see the content of the medical checks
D. there is a legal requirement for the medical exams, therefore you are allowed to check their content

2. The internal audit department sometimes hires an external audit firm to provide audit services. Which of the following is likely true?
A. the external firm, instructed by the internal audit department, is a data processor
B. the lawful processing criterion changes if an external firm is under contract
C. the external firm, instructed by the internal audit department, is a controller
D. consent from the data subjects is required for allowing third parties like the external firm access to the personal data

3. When transferring the employee data to Canada, which of the following is not an appropriate way?
A. Binding Corporate Rules
B. relying on the arrangement struck between countries in the context of the CLOUD Act
C. standard contractual clauses
D. doing nothing, except for entering into a Data Processing Agreement

4. Which of the following is likely not a lawful processing criterion that can be used by the internal audit department?
A. legal obligation
B. legitimate interest
C. consent
D. contract

5. During a privacy audit, the internal audit department discovers that the privacy officer has received a request from a customer to remove his payment data from the company's system (right to be forgotten). The privacy officer refused. Which of the following is likely the reason for refusal?
A. legal obligation
B. legitimate interest
C. extension of the 30 days
D. the customer not being from the European Union

The year is 2017, and you have just started a job as a Data Protection Officer at the national tax agency. You are the successor of the Data Protection Officer that was responsible for checking compliance with Directive 95. She left, however, feeling the pressure of the upcoming General Data Protection Regulation and the eyes of the public being on all government services.

When you arrive on your first day of work, you find out that no steps have been taken to comply with the General Data Protection Regulation yet. According to the information in the handover document of the previous Data Protection Officer, the organization is fully compliant with Directive 95. However, no evidence or trail of assessments of compliance can be found, except for the one-sheet handover document which is not supported by any other documents. You are a disappointed, because the General Data Protection Regulation requires all processing of personal data to be recorded in a register (which is a lot of work).

To learn more about the Data Protection practices at the national tax agency, you conduct interviews with employees of several departments of the organization. Nobody seems to have any useful information for you. When asking the director, she appears not to be aware of how exactly the supposed compliance was achieved, but she does know the organization needs a Data Protection Officer before the General Data Protection Regulation deadline of May 25th 2018.

6. As the new Data Protection Officer, what would you do first?
A. inform the director about the high General Data Protection Regulation fines
B. inform the Data Protection Authority of likely non-compliance
C. hire a Chief Information Security Officer
D. create awareness of the General Data Protection Regulation in the organization

7. Which of the following is least likely missing in the organization?
A. a Data Processing Inventory
B. Data Protection Impact Assessments
C. a lawful processing criterion for all processing of personal data
D. Employee awareness

8. You walk through the office during your first inspection, and you notice a post-it note sticking to the door, containing sensitive personal information about an individual, out in the open for everyone to see. As a Data Protection Officer, what are you required to do here?
A. report the post-it to the employee
B. report the incident as a data breach to the Data Protection Authority
C. nothing, the post-it is outside of the General Data Protection Regulation's scope
D. report the post-it to the director, and if no action is taken bring it under the board of directors' attention during the annual small incidents report

9. What can be said about the organization using the lawful processing criterion *legitimate interest*?
A. for public tasks, the organization is not allowed to use this lawful processing criterion
B. for public tasks, a proper balancing of interests must take place
C. government-funded organizations are never allowed to rely on this lawful processing criterion
D. when using the lawful processing criterion legitimate interest for their legally required tasks, data subjects can stop the processing by objecting

10. After informing the director of the aspects not in compliance yet, the director disagrees with you and chooses to terminate your employment in the probation period. Which of the following is likely true?
A. this termination of employment is not allowed
B. no reason is needed to fire someone in the probation period, hence it is allowed
C. you can report this to the board of directors, resulting in your reinstatement
D. the director has no power to terminate your contract

Your life is getting busier by the day, and the stress from modern-day living is getting you down. Then, unexpectedly, you receive a card from your boss, who wishes you a happy birthday. Initially you are delighted and full of appreciation for your boss, since he remembered your birthday (which you yourself had forgotten due to the stressfulness of life). Then, however, you are filled with more questions than joy, as you have not shared your birthday with any of your co-workers.

The next day you thank your boss for the card, and ask how he found out about your birthday. Your boss says he wishes he could take the credit for the birthday card, because the company receives a lot of positive feedback on them, but that it is actually the personnel department that initiates this gesture for all staff.

When you head over to the personnel department, they inform you that all employee addresses, birthdays, and annual appraisal scores are transferred to an external service that automatically sends out birthday cards to all those employees with a satisfactory score on their appraisal. This is an effort of the company to reward personnel for their hard work, and to raise job satisfaction of the employees it wishes to retain.

11. In this scenario, what can be said about the service that sends the birthday cards?
A. the service is a controller
B. the service can use the data how it wants, until an opt-out is used
C. the service uses the lawful processing criterion *necessary for the performance of a contract*, since it has a contract for its services
D. the service is a processor

12. What can be said about linking the sending of the cards to the appraisal?
A. the company has a legitimate interest in keeping employees happy, hence the approach is justified
B. the transferring of the appraisal score is unnecessary
C. the company has a labor contract with the employee, hence the approach is justified
D. employees are not objecting to the sharing of their data, hence it is an acceptable practice

13. Which of the following is not required in this scenario?
A. Binding Corporate Rules
B. a privacy notice
C. a Data Processing Agreement
D. transparency

14. You request the company to stop sharing employees' appraisal scores with the external service. What is most likely going to happen?
A. the company points out that the Data Protection Authority has issued guidance on similar cases, and it turns out the practice is fine
B. the company will refuse because it thinks what it is doing is acceptable, and you are fully in your right to file a complaint with the Data Protection Authority
C. you talk to the data protection officer about the practice, and he replies that he is fully aware and that the data sharing is proportionate
D. the company tells you it cannot stop sharing the data, but you can opt-out of receiving a birthday card by removing your birthday from the system

15. It turns out the external service is in the US. Which of the following is not required?
A. Binding Corporate Rules
B. a privacy notice
C. a Data Processing Agreement
D. standard contractual clauses

A high school is taking its annual school photo. Most students are excited, but some are insecure about their appearance and only join because they think they have no choice, as well as due to peer pressure from their classmates. For students younger than 16 years of age, the school has asked the parents for permission. All parents have consented to a school photo being taken of their child, and explicitly allowed the photo to be taken and sold to all classmates of their child.

To make use of the social media hype, the school uploads all school photos to its social media page, so all students can tag each other and share the photo on their own social media page as they like. The option to tag is widely used, but most notably misused. One girl is tagged as "Fatty McGee", and a boy wearing a Yarmulke is tagged in an anti-Semitic fashion. The next day, these tags in the photos are used to tease these two particular students.

The school quickly receives requests to remove the tags, but is unable to, because the tags were not placed by the school. As a last resort, the school removes the photos completely, but alas, the photos and their negative tags have spread.

16. What can be said about the school uploading the photos to social media?
A. the uploading to social media is not compatible with the original purpose
B. the school has obtained consent for the photo, and cannot be held responsible for the results of uploading the photo
C. the social media site is fully responsible for what happened with the photo
D. the school is in full compliance

17. The Yarmulke can be linked to religion. What can be said about the student?
A. the photo of the child wearing the Yarmulke contains sensitive personal data, as it exposes the child's religion
B. only the anti-Semitic tags are sensitive personal data, as they explicitly reveal the child's religion
C. unless someone's religion is explicitly mentioned, it should not be considered to be sensitive personal data
D. the Yarmulke does not constitute sensitive personal data, but the size of the girl tagged as "Fatty McGee" is sensitive personal data as it indicates health issues

18. If wearing the Yarmulke were indeed considered as resulting in a photo containing sensitive personal data, what can be said about the processing restrictions?
A. the school photo has to be deleted, since it contains sensitive personal data
B. the child wearing the Yarmulke needs to be blurred to make him unidentifiable
C. the sensitive personal data has been manifestly made public, so there is no processing restriction
D. educational institutions are exempt from the processing restrictions

19. Which of the following is not a risk when uploading the photo to social media?
A. the school loses control and is unaware which processing takes place after uploading
B. the school is sued for processing sensitive personal data
C. the school can be held accountable for the damages caused by uploading the photo
D. after deleting the photo, the social media website still processes the photo further

20. Which of the following can be said about the girl who is made fun of for her weight?

A. weight constitutes sensitive personal data and is not allowed to be processed

B. consent has been obtained, so the uploading is fine even if it is sensitive personal data

C. the girl is younger than 16, so the processing restriction does not apply

D. whether this constitutes sensitive personal data is still unclear, and case law is needed

A well-known hospital, where many celebrities go for their medical treatment and plastic surgery, has been involved in a scandal. After a politician came in, one of the doctors in charge of her treatment was robbed on his way home. Among other things, the folder with hardcopy files he kept in his briefcase was stolen. The hardcopy files contained the notes that he has taken during the treatment of his patients, and the analyses of their illness or treatment.

Upon realizing what he stole, the thief sold the information to a gossip magazine, which published the embarrassing treatment the politician was in the hospital for. The entire country was in shock, and the politician resigned. She lost so much face that she stayed away from the public eye entirely, having to miss the sizeable salary she enjoyed as a politician.

Bringing files home is not explicitly forbidden by the hospital's policies. As a matter of fact, the doctors are not trained in the safe handling of patient files at all. In addition, the entry in the data processing inventory is vague about what exactly is done with the files. You, as an employee of the national Data Protection Authority, have been asked to investigate the situation.

21. What is most likely the first thing you will check after finding out there is no explicit policy in place that covers taking files home?
A. whether the hospital has the required Data Protection Officer
B. whether the required Data Protection Impact Assessment has been performed
C. whether the hospital has had similar incidents in the past
D. whether the doctor's laptop has the required level of security

22. If the hospital has an annual profit of one billion Euros, what is the maximum fine it can receive?
A. 20 million Euros
B. 10 million Euros
C. 2 million Euros
D. 40 million Euros

23. Which of the following is likely not a reason for the hospital to perform a Data Protection Impact Assessment?
A. automated decision-making
B. monitoring of people
C. data of weak data subjects
D. large amounts of data

24. Given that the details were published by the gossip magazine, which of the following is likely true?
A. it constitutes a data breach, but since it already leaked, the data subject does not need to be informed
B. as long as the hospital does not confirm the leak, there is no way of knowing whether the file is accurate, and it is not considered personal data
C. since the breach only concerns one person, the breach does not need to be reported
D. the data subjects need to be informed by the hospital

25. During your investigation you are confronted with the information that all other national hospitals have the same level of protection. What does this likely mean for your case?
A. the current state of technology has to be taken into account, so the hospital is free from blame
B. if the Data Protection Impact Assessment mentions benchmarking with other hospitals, it has done sufficient effort
C. this means your scope is now expanded to all other national hospitals
D. nothing

A large chemical company called *GP Oil* frequently looks for talented staff. To attract this talented staff, GP Oil has an elaborate recruitment and hiring process in place with a flashy website where potential recruits are encouraged to apply for vacant positions. An external firm has set up the entire website's structure, including the flow of documents.

The recruitment process consists of sending a motivation letter, filling out a CV online, several interviews, and a personality test. This ensures only the most suitable and highly qualified candidates are hired, and no employees with undesirable personality traits succeed in the recruitment process. GP Oil sees this as needed to prevent hiring unproductive workers, which are then difficult to get rid of given the local labor laws in some countries.

Not only is the recruitment website great for the help with filling vacancies, it also functions as a place to spark interest. To make everyone feel welcome, vacancies are frequently posted for non-existing posts, in order to give people hope. Nobody is hired, but it does provide a large number of interesting CVs, as well as a collection of test results that can be used to create a blacklist of employees not to hire. For example, candidates for which the result of the personality test shows they are emotionally unstable are automatically ignored during future applications.

26. CVs are automatically scanned for key words and phrases. What is most likely true in this case?
A. this automatic checking is not allowed
B. the privacy notice should mention automatic decision-making
C. candidates are entitled to a non-automated way of checking their CV
D. a CV is considered sensitive personal data, meaning consent is required

27. What is the main issue with the fake vacancies?
A. when the privacy notice states that the position is non-existent, nobody will apply
B. consent is needed to use the CV for other purposes
C. there is no lawful processing criterion for this processing
D. there are no issues

28. When a candidate gets suspicious and requests a copy of his personal data, which of the following is likely true?
A. the fact that the person applied to a fake vacancy can be incriminating, so the company does not have to release that the person applied for that position
B. (at least) all information he sent to the company needs to be provided
C. until the application process is over, no data need to be provided
D. as the lawful processing criterion *performance of contract* is used, no data need to be provided

29. The personality test goes in depth and exposes a lot about the applicant. Which of the following is most likely the smallest risk?
A. when data subjects request access, the full details of the personality test need to be provided
B. the personality test could reveal sensitive personal information
C. the personality test is excessive for the purpose
D. consent is required for the personality test, which cannot be given freely

30. For the CVs that the Human Resource personnel find interesting to store or distribute, which is the most likely practical concern?
A. getting consent to keep the CVs
B. providing a privacy notice when filing an application
C. copies of the CVs spreading uncontrolled through the company
D. deleting applicant data from the system

A video gaming company has sold many copies of a particular video game, which has an option where you can play online with your friends or random strangers. It is massively successful, and millions of people play it on a daily basis, resulting in a large number of recorded gaming sessions appearing on social media.

One negative consequence of its popularity is that video game has been pirated a lot, which is what the company anticipated. In order to make up for losses in sales revenue, it has been decided to gather data through analyzing the cookies on the player's device. This is done by the game software scanning the folders on the user's device where cookies and browsing history are usually stored.

In order to be able to create a profile of the users, the company creates a database of unique device properties with the list of websites that user has visited. The information gathered here is very useful for predicting a user's buying habits and there are a lot of interested marketing companies that pay a high price for the information the video game company provides.

The side-business turns out to be so lucrative that the video game company creates an entire department to experiment with the best ways to collect data and create information to sell. All kinds of tracking technologies are tested on the users of the video game, even an analysis tool that can see whether a user has a certain cognitive condition based on the way he/she plays the video game, or whether the user is employed based on the amount of time the video game is played.

31. What can be said about the data collection?
A. as long as the software is downloaded illegally, the practice is fine
B. secret data collection is not allowed in this case
C. browsing history is not personal data, so it is allowed
D. making up for lost profits weighs heavy on the legitimate interest balance

32. The company revises its privacy policy, and users now have to consent to this data collection before being able to play the game. What is the most likely reason the consent will be invalid?
A. the consent will not be clear
B. the consent will not be freely given
C. the consent will not be specific
D. the consent will not be reversible

33. After the financial losses have become significant, the company bans users that have pirated the game. It does so based on the serial number on the user's device. What can be said about this practice?
A. the serial number of a device can be considered personal data if it can be traced back to someone
B. the serial number of a device only says something about a device and is not personal data
C. no information about what is being linked to a serial number is necessary in a privacy notice
D. the company can refuse users access to the information linked to the serial number of their device

34. When the company collects data about users in order to sell those data, what is the company?
A. a processor if it has not yet found a buyer
B. a controller if it has not yet found a buyer
C. always a processor
D. neither a processor not a controller until a buyer is found

35. Whenever a user achieves a high score, the user can choose to upload it to the company's server so that it is visible for other users. What is required in this case?
A. consent
B. legitimate interest
C. a privacy notice
D. a Data Processing Agreement

A logistics company operating from a massive warehouse has recently been the victim of theft. Some of the more valuable shipments have been stolen from the warehouse. These shipments contained popular video game consoles and flat screen TVs, and are now being kept in the high value area, for which access is granted only to foremen.

As another measure to prevent future theft of shipments, the logistics company plans to install CCTV cameras in the warehouse. This way, the warehouse can be monitored 24 hours a day, so that regardless of when the theft occurs, it will be recorded on video. A nice High Definition CCTV camera is being used, as this provides for proper identification in case of theft.

Before installing the CCTV cameras, the works council is asked for advice. The works council is always involved when changes happen that affect the work or business, and it is even legally required to give advice on any changes. As expected, the works council rejects the idea and its advice is negative.

As the works council only gives non-binding advice, the company goes ahead and installs the CCTV cameras. Every area of the warehouse is now being monitored 24 hours a day, including during office hours when workers are present in the warehouse.

36. What is most likely the criticism of the works council?
A. CCTV is too expensive for the amount stolen, and other ways are recommended
B. the works council says that under no circumstances can CCTV be justifiable at the place where workers load the truck
C. the logistics company first needs to exhaust other means before resorting to CCTV
D. a pay increase is needed to compensate for the decrease in privacy

37. What would be the most acceptable motivation for installing CCTV?
A. it is too costly to track shipments in the warehouse and identify where the shipments were taken
B. GPS tracking of packages at risk is too privacy invasive
C. it has been established that someone sneaked into the warehouse during office hours to steal the shipments
D. in addition to detecting theft, it allows for monitoring compliance with other company rules

38. It has been established that the theft likely occurred at night when no workers were (supposed to be) present in the warehouse. Which of the following most appropriately describes the situation?
A. CCTV can be installed, buy only activated outside of office hours
B. CCTV is allowed to be active the entire day, as it is still possible workers have stolen shipments as well
C. the employer can force workers to consent to CCTV monitoring
D. if the works council agrees, CCTV is allowed

39. When installing CCTV, which of the following is required?
A. a clearly visible sign with information regarding the CCTV
B. a privacy notice posted on the employee board in the cafeteria, visible for everyone
C. a privacy notice by e-mail, which every employee needs to consent to
D. a consent form

40. What is an important consideration when receiving data access requests?
A. the effort to provide someone access to CCTV is disproportionate
B. passport and one other form of ID are needed, to be provided in person
C. balance the interests of the person requesting access with the other person(s) visible
D. CCTV images can be deleted when a person requests access

A small paper company called *Dunder M* has hired you as a Data Protection officer. Their main activity is to sell paper to other businesses, not to individuals. As such, they do not target individual consumers but have a sales team that contacts the potential customers by calling the phone number that is listed on the potential customer's website. Usually this leads to a receptionist who transfers the call to the right person.

Recently it has been the victim of a cyber attack. At first, it suspected the refrigerator company next door to have pulled a digital prank, but soon it found out the cyber attack was serious. All computers are locked by ransomware, and a message is displayed that the data has been copied to a secure location and it will get the data back if a ransom fee is paid.

Although the ransom fee will mean that there will be no budget for the annual bonus, the CEO of Dunder M is desperate and considers paying the perpetrators, by transferring Bitcoin. After consulting the corporate head office, it is decided to pay the ransom. The data, however, are never returned, and all employees are unable to work without their data.

41. As a Data Protection Officer, what is your first priority?
A. reporting the incident to the Data Protection Authority
B. informing the CEO
C. finding out what data have leaked
D. paying the ransom fee

42. In which case would the incident likely not be considered a data breach?
A. if no backup is available
B. if the hard drives are only encrypted
C. if the data are transmitted to the secure location in encrypted form
D. if the information contains only business contacts

43. Which of the following statements is most correct?
A. the Data Protection Officer has 72 hours to report the data breach if it meets the conditions
B. the Chief Information Security Officer determines whether it is a breach that has to be reported
C. all data breaches need to be reported if personal data are involved
D. the organization has 72 hours to report the data breach if it meets the conditions

44. What if no personal data were accessed by the cyber attackers, but all data were lost?
A. if no backup exists, it is still a data breach
B. the incident does not have to be reported
C. the incident is not considered a data breach
D. data subjects do not need to be informed

45. Which of the following would most likely result in Dunder M informing the data subjects?
A. if all phone numbers of the business contacts were leaked
B. if financial data of customers were leaked
C. data subject do not need to be informed, since Dunder M only deals with businesses
D. if employee files were leaked

A marketing company named *Trend Analysis Digital* offers several services. First, it offers to send out mass e-mails to a list of recipients provided by the customer. Second, it offers a survey service, where it contacts persons based on a list provided by the customer or the description of the category of persons described by the customer. Third, it offers a web analysis service where browsing habits of individuals are monitored. All of these services are available to any organization, and are tailored to the customer's needs.

Trend Analysis Digital's first customer in 2019 is an online retailer that sells sneakers. The retailer would like to know who its customers are and what its customers think of the services it provides. Trend Analysis Digital designs a package of services for the retailer, which includes a survey for his customers and an analysis of what type of people the retailer's customers are.

The data that are collected are not stored under any name, but are only given a unique ID. Attached to this ID are the data, such as browsing habits/history, preferences, submitted survey results, etc. If available, an e-mail address is also stored under the profile, in case Trend Analysis Digital would like to contact that person because he/she fits a profile for which it has have a survey.

46. If an e-mail is sent out with a survey after a product is ordered from the retailer's website, which of the following is needed?
A. an opt-out only
B. consent and a discount
C. a web beacon
D. parental consent for minors

47. If Trend Analysis Digital uses a social media web beacon to link the visitor to a social media profile to see which type of people buy from the website, which of the following is most likely used?
A. legitimate interest
B. opt-out
C. consent
D. performance of a contract

48. For the survey, the online retailer offers a 5 Euro discount on the next purchase if the customer's data can be used. Which of the following is most true?
A. by providing a 5 Euro discount, the legitimate interest lawful processing criterion can be applicable
B. by providing a 5 Euro discount, the legal obligation lawful processing criterion can be applicable
C. the consent is not valid if the use of non-anonymous survey data is a condition for the 5 Euro discount
D. once consent has been provided for the survey data, the consent is irreversible

49. For every marketing e-mail sent out, there are tracking technologies that record what the recipient does with the content. Which of the following is most likely true?
A. if the tracking technologies do not allow for anonymous data collection, these tracking technologies are not allowed to be used
B. unless the data are collected without being able to identify the person, consent is the only valid lawful processing criterion
C. when a data subject requests erasure of all his/her data, it is not sufficient to irreversibly remove his/her name and other identifiers from the data set
D. if the data subjects did not opt-out, the tracking technologies are allowed to be used

50. Since the web beacon is technically loaded from a third party, what can be said about the requirement for a privacy notice?
A. the third party is fully responsible for providing a privacy notice
B. even though it is a third-party web beacon, what happens still needs to be mentioned in the privacy notice
C. the website is not responsible for providing a privacy notice for the web beacon
D. although responsible for providing a privacy notice, it is practically impossible to do so, hence there is an exemption

Turbulent Assessments, a company that gathers and analyzes public data on any person, has become quite popular. The service started two years ago, right after several terrorists turned out to have infiltrated a large multinational to use its recourses for their cause.

The way Turbulent Assessments works, is that its customers submit the name of the person they want screened, after which its software scrapes the internet for that person's personal data. The software then creates a predictive psychiatric evaluation, allowing the customer access into the prediction of that person's behavior. This can be used for a variety of purposes, such as screening job applicants to see whether he/she fits the department or the screening of compatibility of potential spouses.

Being incredibly successful, Turbulent Assessments has received a lot media attention. This media attention has also led to scrutiny by the Data Protection Authority. No violation has been established yet, but Turbulent Assessments has received a request for information, and it appears to be quite time consuming to respond to the request in a timely fashion. Turbulent Assessments has responded to the Data Protection Authority that the request for information may be somewhat unrealistic and asked whether it can get an extension of the deadline.

51. In this scenario, which statement is not applicable to Turbulent Assessments?
A. if Turbulent Assessments performs its analysis to screen potential job applicants, it requires a Data Processing Agreement
B. Turbulent Assessments requires a lawful processing criterion to process the public data
C. any individual using the services of Turbulent assessments is outside of the scope of the General Data Protection Regulation
D. all data used by Turbulent Assessments are public, so they are outside of the scope of the General Data Protection Regulation

52. If Turbulent Assessments stores its data scrapings (so not the analysis results) using a cloud service, which of the following is applicable?
A. no extra safeguards are required, as it only concerns public data
B. no lawful processing criterion is needed, as it concerns public data and thus in line with the original processing purpose
C. a Data Processing Agreement is required
D. data breaches have no consequences for public data

53. Which of the following is most likely true regarding Turbulent assessment's obligations to comply with any request from the Data Protection Authority?
A. since the analyzed data are public, all Turbulent Assessments' activities are acceptable
B. Turbulent Assessments has to cooperate
C. no new personal data are generated during Turbulent Assessments' work, so there will be no contact with the Data Protection Authority
D. Turbulent Assessments only needs to cooperate if a data breach occurs

54. When Jack receives a rejection from a company where he applied for a job, and it motivates the rejection with a negative public assessment, which of the following is most likely not true?
A. the company was supposed to inform Jack that the assessment was part of the procedure
B. consent would have been invalid
C. the employer is the Data Processor
D. the employer is the controller

55. Which of the following statements is most likely true regarding Turbulent Assessments?

A. depending on the context, they can be either Data Controller or Data Processor

B. Turbulent Assessments is always responsible for providing the data subject a privacy notice

C. when Turbulent Assessments moves to the US it will immediately fall out of the General Data Protection Regulation's scope

D. Turbulent Assessments is exempt from the access request obligation, as it concerns public data so the data subject has full access already

Brendon, an ex-employee of a Dutch University, is curious about the personal data his previous employer still processes. It has been three years since he left, and he starts with consulting the privacy notice posted on the University's website. The privacy notice has changed quite a bit since Brendon worked at the University, so it takes him a while to go through all the information.

According to the most recent privacy notice, the way to receive a copy of your personal data is by submitting a request to the University's Data Protection Officer. Brendon sends an e-mail to the University's Data Protection Officer to request a copy of his personal data. The Data Protection Officer at the University receives the request and, somewhat disgruntled, starts the process of gathering the personal data of Brendon.

All relevant persons at the University are informed of the request. One department however, informs the Data Protection Officer that it has personal data of Brendon, but will not be handing over a copy of the data. The department claims it does not have to, which the Data Protection Officer is then asked to assess. After assessing the situation, the Data Protection Officer concludes that the University is indeed not required to hand over these data to Brendon.

56. When receiving Brendon's request for access to his personal data, what is most likely the University's first reaction?
A. ask Brendon for a reasonable fee for the access to his data
B. ask Brendon to identify himself
C. inform Brendon his request is too large, and that the University wishes to extend the period of responding
D. tell Brendon that he had the chance to access his data at the time he was employed at the University, meaning the University is not required to comply with his request

57. Regarding the time to react to Brendon's access request, which of the following is correct?
A. the University can immediately inform Brendon that his request will take longer than the 30 days
B. the University has 20 days to respond to Brendon's request
C. the University has 30 days to respond to Brendon's request
D. none of the answers are correct

58. The department that processes Brendon's personal data and refuses to provide Brendon with access is most likely which of the following?
A. a science department
B. the legal department
C. human resources
D. medical services

59. The University responds to Brendon with the remark that it does still have Brendon's data in its system, but that it is not processing the data, and hence denies Brendon access to his data. Which of the following statement is correct?
A. storing is not processing, hence Brendon can be denied access
B. storing is also processing, hence not a reason to deny Brendon access
C. Brian consented to the storage of his data, which result in a waiving of access rights
D. Brendon has full access rights to the stored data

60. After a lot of hassle Brendon gains access to part of the data the University stores on him. He finds out part of it is embarrassing and tells the University to delete it. Which of the following is true in this case?
A. the right to be forgotten is an absolute right, so the University must comply
B. the right to be forgotten outweighs any lawful processing criterion the University can have, so the University needs to comply
C. the University does not need to comply, since Brendon is no longer a University employee
D. if the University has a legal reason to keep the data on Brendon, it may keep the data

You have just fallen ill, in the sense that you have an embarrassing issue for which you do not wish to consult a medical practitioner. Instead, you turn to the internet and order the medication you think you need, from the *Pharmacy of Canada*. The online pharmacy seems reliable, as you can pay in Euro and select your local language.

When you receive the medication you decide not to use it, after you balance out the risks of self-prescribed medication with the medical condition that may or may not be real. You throw the suspicious looking package with medication in the trash and forget about the whole situation. And, a few days later, your condition disappears, comforting you in having taken the right decision regarding the use of the medication.

Then, after some months, you receive a phone call, asking if you are interested in cheap erectile dysfunction pills. This is completely unrelated to the medication you ordered in the past. On top of that the phone call is unwanted and you had forgotten all about the order you placed. You ask the caller to never call you again, because if you need something you will call. From the caller's response it is unclear whether the caller will comply with your request.

61. Which if the following is likely true regarding the website?
A. the Canadian website falls outside of the scope of the General Data Protection Regulation
B. the website is based outside the European Union, and the data need to be handled compliant with the General Data Protection Regulation
C. the General Data Protection Regulation does not apply, because the website does not contain information on natural persons from the European Union
D. only the e-privacy directive is relevant in this case

62. In order to contact you by phone, which of the following was likely needed?
A. consent was required
B. nothing was required, as you are customer
C. freely given consent was required
D. the opportunity to have opted out

63. Which of the following can be said about the type of data the website handles?
A. buying certain medication can be seen as sensitive personal data
B. the website handles orders, not personal data
C. medication is always considered sensitive personal data
D. there is no certainty the medication is actually used, so there are no sensitive personal data involved

64. All of a sudden you see an advertisement on social media, with the medication you ordered from the online pharmacy. Which of the following could most likely be true?
A. the website has processed your data without a valid lawful processing criterion
B. social media sites sniff your device for invoices
C. your key strokes were logged by the social media site
D. you consented to being shown advertisement based on cookies placed by other websites

65. If the company turns out the be from within the European Union, which of the following is likely true?
A. no intercontinental laws apply
B. an opt-out at the time of sale was needed
C. no Data Protection Impact Assessment is needed
D. Binding Corporate Rules are necessary

You just started a new job, as Data Protection Officer of a video streaming service. Ever since the video streaming service started, you have been a big fan. You really feel like it is a company that contributes to the flourishing of society by allowing users to share content with everyone who is interested.

The first day on the job you start meeting your colleagues, but most importantly you inspect the personal data processing inventory. Your idea of a prudent first day is to know the processes so you can ask whoever you speak to about the processes he or she is responsible for. Going through the personal data processing inventory, you see a lot of red flags. Many processes seem to be secretive and unnecessary for the services the customers buy.

One example is secretly keeping track of the viewing history, and placing the person in a category. These data are then used to recommend shows to that user. Where you first thought that these recommendations were a friendly service to the user, you now find out they are based on what the producing company of a TV show is paying the streaming service to recommend to, for example, a single white heterosexual male.

66. What is likely the biggest reason the identified red flag will lead to uncovering a non-compliant practice?
A. the labeling is not needed to provide the service the customers pay for
B. the categories attached to a user contain sensitive personal information
C. there is no non-compliance, the legitimate interest criterion is applicable
D. it is forbidden to process sensitive personal information

67. What is not a task of the Data Protection Officer?
A. inform the CEO
B. instruct management to reprimand the employee responsible
C. educate the organization
D. give negative advice regarding the situation

68. If a data subject requests access to his/her data, which of the following is not true?
A. the data not provided by the data subject, do not need to be provided
B. Binding Corporate Rules in place will not prevent access to data stored outside of the European Union
C. the CEO has final say in whether the data subject is provided access
D. the data subject does not need to show a valid form of ID

69. Which of the following would you expect to find for the process of placing customers in categories?
A. separate servers for category data
B. a Data Protection Impact Assessment
C. a category is not personal data
D. CEO approval

70. Which of the following is likely true for the customers outside of the European Union?
A. unless Binding Corporate Rules are in place, a Data Processing Agreement needs to be in place
B. HIPAA preempts the General Data Protection Regulation
C. unless citizens outside the European Union are specifically targeted, they do not fall within the scope of the General Data Protection Regulation
D. they require the same protection as citizens from the European Union

On a nice and sunny day, you decide to visit an amusement park with your friends for a day of fun and excitements, riding roller coasters and other rides. The most spectacular ride, a giant roller coaster called *The Goliath*, is the most popular of all. You and your friends spend half of the day riding it.

At end of the day, on your way home, your friends discuss the day. During the discussion a remark is made about how it looked like your glasses were almost flying off on the last picture. With an awkward smile on your face, you ask "who took a picture?". Your friends react surprised to you not having seen the photos displayed when exiting the ride. You actually did not recognize those as being taken that day, and your eyes were closed at the moments the pictures were taken.

Although you are not happy with being photographed without permission, you do understand that it is part of the business model of the amusement park and that it is quite common to take photos during a roller coaster ride. You would have liked to have had the opportunity to see the photo and be able to purchase it. When you arrive home you decide to send an e-mail to the amusement park about it, requesting a copy of the photo.

71. How should you have found out about the photo?
A. the photo is being deleted, so informing the person afterward is sufficient
B. you should have been provided with the option to consent to the photo, or not go on the roller coaster
C. you should have been informed right after entering the amusement park
D. before taking the photo, you should have been informed

72. When you get home it does not sit well with you that the amusement park has taken your photo without asking for your permission. You send an access request. What is likely true for the access request?
A. the company needs to send you all your personal data, including the photo if they still have it
B. the photo also contains other people, and therefore can be withheld during an access request
C. since the amusement park took the photo to sell, it can charge a fee for it
D. the amusement park can send you your data without the photo, if it informs you the photo is visible in the amusement park itself

73. If the amusement park wishes to use the photo for its website, which of the following is likely true?
A. the photo falls under the exemption for journalism and can be freely used
B. a fee needs to be paid for the use of the photo
C. the amusement park needs to obtain consent, even if it does not know who the persons in the photo are
D. the amusement park can rely on the legitimate interest lawful processing criterion

74. After sending an access request, you find out the amusement park keeps the photo in a backup in case a visitor wants to order another copy. You request the deletion of your photo, but the amusement park refuses. Which of the following is likely not true?
A. the amusement park needs to crop you out of the photo
B. the amusement park can rely on the legitimate interest lawful processing criterion, as it would be too much work to crop the photo
C. the amusement park should not have kept the photo
D. the amusement park has not obtained valid consent

75. After your access request, you receive a weekly newsletter, as it turns out the amusement park has placed the e-mail address you used for the access request on a mailing list. Which of the following is likely true?
A. until you opt-out, it is allowed to keep you on the mailing list
B. the amusement park needs to provide an opt-out with their newsletter
C. you have visited the park and did not opt-out, so the amusement park has compliantly placed you on the mailing list
D. an e-mail address is not personal data, since anyone can choose any e-mail address

An energy company deals with frequent phone communication. Although the company has a website, most people cannot figure out the solution quickly enough or cannot spare the effort. For that reason, the energy company employs a large team of phone operators that are standing by 24 hours a day to assist customers with any questions or issues.

Dealing with customers on the phone is quite complicated and stressful. Many phone operators make mistakes, resulting in angry customers. The angry customers, in return, cause a large amount of psychological stress, resulting in staff with a burnout and other mental health issues.

For that reason, the energy company has created an elaborate training program. All phone calls are recorded, analyzed and used for training if something can be learned from it. These lessons learned are then used to train new and current phone operators, allowing for continuous improvement.

The company plays an automatic recording at the beginning of any phone call that mentions "this phone call can be recorded for training purposes". This brings the recording to the customer's attention and allows the customer to hang up the phone if he or she does not want to be recorded, hence fulfilling the obligation to inform customers about the processing of their data.

76. What can be said about the message about recording the phone call?
A. if the recording is indeed used for training, the information is not sufficient
B. the information is sufficient, since the recording starts after the message
C. data subjects provide consent by continuing the conversation after the recording
D. the information is not sufficient

77. One of the data subjects is quite annoyed by the recording, and objects to it. Which of the following is most likely true?
A. the recording cannot be stopped and the objection is not valid
B. if the energy company has a legal duty record verbal contracts, the objection will not stand
C. if the Binding Corporate Rules state that phone calls are recorded, the objection will be invalid
D. the privacy notice on the energy company's website explains the process in detail, hence the data subject cannot object

78. If a data subject requests access, does the energy company have to provide the voice recording of the customer?
A. no, as the recording also contains the phone operator's voice
B. no, as sending the recording is disproportionate
C. yes, access needs to be provided
D. the energy company will only be obliged to provide the recording if the customer provides a storage medium for the recording

79. What can be said about the recorded message if the phone operators are located outside of the European Union?
A. the privacy notice on the website will need to be updated so that calling customers know their data are recorded outside of the European Union
B. safeguards need to be in place
C. customers need to provide additional consent
D. the General Data Protection Regulation no longer applies

80. The energy company uses smart meters, that automatically create an energy profile of the customer. Which is likely true?
A. the processing beyond the used energy goes beyond the purpose for which it was collected
B. the smart meters are illegal
C. the customer does not have to consent to receiving an energy profile report
D. no processing beyond the original scope is allowed

You are working for an internationally operating social media website, targeting users all over the globe. Millions of users make use of the website on a daily basis, and large amounts of personal data are stored all over the world on cloud services and private servers.

To access their data, data subjects only have to log on and click the "download my data" button. All the data they uploaded to the website is then packaged in a compressed folder and through a link it can be copied to their local device. The whole process goes automatically, and takes only a few hours.

Identification is done through logging on, and to prevent anyone from taking over the account when the user is not looking or is automatically logged on, the link to the collection of data is sent only to the e-mail address used to create the social media account.

Then, one day, the Data Protection Officer receives a data access request by telephone. The user says she has lost her password, user name and e-mail account used for her social media account, but would still like to get a copy of her data. All options for recovering the password the conventional way are impossible, and it appears a decision needs to be made regarding the access request.

81. What is likely true for this access request?
A. as she uploaded the data herself, she already has access to the data, and a copy does not have to be provided
B. the personal data, including the website script, need to be provided
C. the social media website needs to also provide the revenue it makes of its users
D. a copy of the personal data has to be provided

82. What can be said about identification before providing any personal data?
A. no identification is required, as she uploaded the data herself
B. only a personal visit showing a valid passport or national ID is sufficient
C. a video call could be sufficient
D. providing a new e-mail address, so the account can be reset, is sufficient

83. Which of the following is likely not true about data subject identification?
A. not requiring identification leaves the risk of giving the wrong person access to someone's data
B. sending the password and user name by post is a reliable way of providing only the right person with access
C. using a known e-mail address or phone number for verification is a reliable way for the social media site to verify
D. the social media website needs the highest possible level of certainty in the identification

84. The social media site does not only keep data that the users provided themselves. Which of the following is likely true?
A. there is no possible lawful processing criterion for this practice
B. since the social media site is used free of charge, the practice is justified
C. if the users did not provide the data themselves, they are not personal data
D. all personal data need to be provided

85. The social media site allows other websites to use the social media site's web beacon so it can store which websites are visited by the users of the social media site. What can be said about this practice?
A. it does not result in personal data, since a visited website is not a natural person
B. as long as the collected data are not used for advertisement, it falls outside of the scope of the e-privacy directive
C. it is deceiving and difficult to implement legally
D. although personal data, the social media site can use *legitimate interest* to not have to notify users of the data collection

Traffic in the city is getting worse and worse. Commuters are frustrated and tourists prefer a less crowded city. Accidents are also occurring more and more often, especially given the number of international workers who are used to a different way of driving.

Then, one day, you see a large number of scoot vehicles spread throughout the city. These vehicles are placed there by a company called *EZ Scoot*, in an effort to reduce car traffic in the city. The vehicles are small and easy to use, allowing the young and hip people, as well as the old and rusty people, to go to work or go to their favorite avocado restaurant.

In order to use the scoot vehicles you have to install an application on your phone and scan the code of the scoot vehicle. The vehicle is then unlocked, and your account will be charged for the time you use it. Of course, to prevent theft, all scoot vehicles emit a GPS signal which EZ Scoot can access whenever it wants. If a vehicle has not been used for a certain period of time, someone is sent to the location where it has been left to check on the vehicle. Most of the times it has been damaged, but other times it has been taken into someone's home.

86. What can be said about the GPS signal?
A. the GPS data are personal data
B. the GPS data are not personal data
C. the GPS data could be personal data
D. no information is collected

87. Which further processing would most likely not fit the purpose?
A. selling data for the most visited places to a marketing company
B. optimizing traffic based on the places most travelled through
C. storing the GPS data linked to the users
D. sending the coordinates of a stolen scoot vehicle located in a residence to the police

88. What can be done to ensure the GPS signal is not personal data?
A. unlink beginning and end location from profiles
B. restrict the area in which GPS signals are tracked
C. only store usernames, not actual names
D. do not store any type of name

89. If a scoot device is stolen, the data are sent to the police. What can be said about this practice?
A. an unacceptable practice
B. the GPS data are not personal data
C. the police will not take any action, as they are not allowed to process the personal data
D. likely an acceptable practice

90. You use a scoot vehicle every now and then, and request EZ scoot to sent you a copy of your personal data. Which of the following is likely true?
A. GPS data are not personal data, so no data need to be provided
B. only financial transaction data need to be provided
C. you only have the right to be forgotten, not the right to access
D. whatever EZ scoot stores about you, has to be provided

CORRECT ANSWERS:

1C	24D	47C	70D
2A	25D	48C	71D
3B	26B	49B	72A
4C	27C	50B	73C
5A	28B	51D	74B
6D	29A	52C	75B
7C	30C	53B	76D
8C	31B	54C	77B
9A	32B	55A	78C
10A	33A	56B	79B
11D	34B	57C	80A
12B	35C	58A	81D
13A	36C	59B	82C
14B	37C	60D	83B
15A	38A	61B	84D
16A	39A	62D	85C
17A	40C	63A	86C
18C	41C	64A	87C
19B	42B	65B	88B
20D	43D	66B	89D
21B	44A	67B	90D
22D	45D	68A	
23A	46D	69B	

EXPLANATIONS:

Midway through your career, you find yourself working for the internal audit department of a large manufacturing company. The company produces mechanical parts, which it ships to Canada, where the parts are assembled into ships. All employee data are shared between the European Union and Canada, because half of the work takes place in the European Union and other half in Canada. This is needed to ensure that all employees are paid and the files of all employees are updated as needed.

The internal audit department performs compliance audits, verifying whether all practices of the company are compliant with legislation and company policy. In the previous years, there have been several severe accidents in organizations with similar activities, therefore a lot of focus is placed on Health & Safety in the manufacturing process. As part of the audit schedule, you perform a Health & Safety audit, since Health & Safety is now high on the company's agenda and the industry is highly regulated.

When you are at the European manufacturing location, you want to check whether all employees have undergone their legally required medical check. This leads to some meddling from the works council. The works council is upset about some of the information that is required for providing assurance that the company complies with the Health & Safety regulations.

1. Which of the following is most likely the case?
A. information on whether a check was performed is sensitive personal data, and consent is needed
B. you are not allowed to perform your check, as it concerns sensitive personal data, and consent cannot be freely given in this scenario
C. you are allowed to check all the documents you want, as you do not need to see the content of the medical checks (correct)
D. there is a legal requirement for the medical exams, therefore you are allowed to check their content

Explanation: C is the correct answer, since the results of a medical check are sensitive personal data, but not the fact that a medical check has been performed. A and B are wrong because it is not sensitive personal data, and D is incorrect because this does not mean you can check the content.

2. The internal audit department sometimes hires an external audit firm to provide audit services. Which of the following is likely true?
A. the external firm, instructed by the internal audit department, is a data processor (correct)
B. the lawful processing criterion changes if an external firm is under contract
C. the external firm, instructed by the internal audit department, is a controller
D. consent from the data subjects is required for allowing third parties like the external firm access to the personal data
Explanation: A is the correct answer, because the external firm is a processor due to only doing what the audit department instructs it to.

3. When transferring the employee data to Canada, which of the following is not an appropriate way?
A. Binding Corporate Rules
B. relying on the arrangement struck between countries in the context of the CLOUD Act (correct)
C. standard contractual clauses
D. doing nothing, except for entering into a Data Processing Agreement
Explanation: A, C, and D are valid ways. Even D would be fine for the processors, since Canada is (partly) adequate. B does not arrange any agreements on how to handle the personal data, so is the correct answer.

4. Which of the following is likely not a lawful processing criterion that can be used by the internal audit department?
A. legal obligation
B. legitimate interest
C. consent (correct)
D. contract

Explanation: consent is not needed for an audit, as some audits are required by law, some are for the good of the company and some could be to make sure your labor contract is fully complied with. D may be a bit of a stretch, but C is the most unlikely because consent is likely not freely given.

5. During a privacy audit, the internal audit department discovers that the privacy officer has received a request from a customer to remove his payment data from the company's system (right to be forgotten). The privacy officer refused. Which of the following is likely the reason for refusal?
A. legal obligation (correct)
B. legitimate interest
C. extension of the 30 days
D. the customer not being from the European Union
Explanation: If a company has a legal obligation to keep data, such as invoices for fiscal reasons, then the right to be forgotten cannot be fully executed, so A is the correct answer.

The year is 2017, and you have just started a job as a Data Protection Officer at the national tax agency. You are the successor of the Data Protection Officer that was responsible for checking compliance with Directive 95. She left, however, feeling the pressure of the upcoming General Data Protection Regulation and the eyes of the public being on all government services.

When you arrive on your first day of work, you find out that no steps have been taken to comply with the General Data Protection Regulation yet. According to the information in the handover document of the previous Data Protection Officer, the organization is fully compliant with Directive 95. However, no evidence or trail of assessments of compliance can be found, except for the one-sheet handover document which is not supported by any other documents. You are a disappointed, because the General Data Protection Regulation requires all processing of personal data to be recorded in a register (which is a lot of work).

To learn more about the Data Protection practices at the national tax agency, you conduct interviews with employees of several departments of the organization. Nobody seems to have any useful information for you. When asking the director, she appears not to be aware of how exactly the supposed compliance was achieved, but she does know the organization needs a Data Protection Officer before the General Data Protection Regulation deadline of May 25th 2018.

6. As the new Data Protection Officer, what would you do first?
A. inform the director about the high General Data Protection Regulation fines
B. inform the Data Protection Authority of likely non-compliance
C. hire a Chief Information Security Officer
D. create awareness of the General Data Protection Regulation in the organization (correct)
Explanation: Awareness is the first step to compliance, as in the case of this organization you will not get all the information you need to create a plan towards compliance if there is no awareness. D is the correct answer. The other three can be useful, but answer D has the highest impact at this stage.

7. Which of the following is least likely missing in the organization?
A. a Data Processing Inventory
B. Data Protection Impact Assessments
C. a lawful processing criterion for all processing of personal data (correct)
D. Employee awareness
Explanation: if Directive 95 is complied with, all processing of personal data has a lawful processing criterion. The lawful processing criteria have not changed much since Directive 95, so C is the correct answer. All the others are likely missing, as no start has been made towards compliance with the new regulation.

8. You walk through the office during your first inspection, and you notice a post-it note sticking to the door, containing sensitive personal information about an individual, out in the open for everyone to see. As a Data Protection Officer, what are you required to do here?
A. report the post-it to the employee
B. report the incident as a data breach to the Data Protection Authority
C. nothing, the post-it is outside of the General Data Protection Regulation's scope (correct)
D. report the post-it to the director, and if no action is taken bring it under the board of directors' attention during the annual small incidents report
Explanation: the post-it falls outside of the scope of the regulation, as it is not automated processing or part of a filing system. C is the correct answer.

9. What can be said about the organization using the lawful processing criterion *legitimate interest*?
A. for public tasks, the organization is not allowed to use this lawful processing criterion (correct)
B. for public tasks, a proper balancing of interests must take place
C. government-funded organizations are never allowed to rely on this lawful processing criterion
D. when using the lawful processing criterion legitimate interest for their legally required tasks, data subjects can stop the processing by objecting

Explanation: government organizations cannot rely on legitimate interest for their public tasks, so A is the correct answer. B implies using legitimate interest, C is not true as it is only for public tasks, and D is wrong because objecting has no effect if something is legally required (imagine objecting to processing your personal data needed for you to pay taxes).

10. After informing the director of the aspects not in compliance yet, the director disagrees with you and chooses to terminate your employment in the probation period. Which of the following is likely true?

A. this termination of employment is not allowed (correct)
B. no reason is needed to fire someone in the probation period, hence it is allowed
C. you can report this to the board of directors, resulting in your reinstatement
D. the director has no power to terminate your contract
Explanation: it seems the termination is due to a disagreement, which means A is the correct answer because to secure a Data Protection Officer's independence he/she cannot be punished his/her interpretation of the regulation.

Your life is getting busier by the day, and the stress from modern-day living is getting you down. Then, unexpectedly, you receive a card from your boss, who wishes you a happy birthday. Initially you are delighted and full of appreciation for your boss, since he remembered your birthday (which you yourself had forgotten due to the stressfulness of life). Then, however, you are filled with more questions than joy, as you have not shared your birthday with any of your co-workers.

The next day you thank your boss for the card, and ask how he found out about your birthday. Your boss says he wishes he could take the credit for the birthday card, because the company receives a lot of positive feedback on them, but that it is actually the personnel department that initiates this gesture for all staff.

When you head over to the personnel department, they inform you that all employee addresses, birthdays, and annual appraisal scores are transferred to an external service that automatically sends out birthday cards to all those employees with a satisfactory score on their appraisal. This is an effort of the company to reward personnel for their hard work, and to raise job satisfaction of the employees it wishes to retain.

11. In this scenario, what can be said about the service that sends the birthday cards?
A. the service is a controller
B. the service can use the data how it wants, until an opt-out is used
C. the service uses the lawful processing criterion *necessary for the performance of a contract*, since it has a contract for its services
D. the service is a processor (correct)
Explanation: the birthday card company processes the data at the request of the company you work for, so can be said to be a data processor. D is the correct answer. A is wrong, B, and C are nonsense.

12. What can be said about linking the sending of the cards to the appraisal?
A. the company has a legitimate interest in keeping employees happy, hence the approach is justified
B. the transferring of the appraisal score is unnecessary (correct)
C. the company has a labor contract with the employee, hence the approach is justified
D. employees are not objecting to the sharing of their data, hence it is an acceptable practice
Explanation: in order to send a birthday card based on an appraisal score, the company you work for does not have to share your appraisal. If it just shares who gets a card, that is sufficient. Transferring the appraisal is excessive sharing of data for achieving the goal (sending a birthday card to high performers), hence B is the correct answer.

13. Which of the following is not required in this scenario?
A. Binding Corporate Rules (correct)
B. a privacy notice
C. a Data Processing Agreement
D. transparency
Explanation: Binding Corporate Rules have no effect on the birthday card company since it is a different company. A is the correct answer, and B, C, and D are required.

14. You request the company to stop sharing employees' appraisal scores with the external service. What is most likely going to happen?
A. the company points out that the Data Protection Authority has issued guidance on similar cases, and it turns out the practice is fine
B. the company will refuse because it thinks what it is doing is acceptable, and you are fully in your right to file a complaint with the Data Protection Authority (correct)
C. you talk to the data protection officer about the practice, and he replies that he is fully aware and that the data sharing is proportionate
D. the company tells you it cannot stop sharing the data, but you can opt-out of receiving a birthday card by removing your birthday from the system

Explanation: as the company seems to think that what it is doing is acceptable, option B is the most likely answer. A is very unlikely, C is very unlikely, and D is improbably as removing your data from the system would likely cause issues in the company's administration. Questions with answers that all seem wrong will be part of the exam, so learn to rank answers from worst to least bad to pick the correct one.

15. It turns out the external service is in the US. Which of the following is not required?
A. Binding Corporate Rules (correct)
B. a privacy notice
C. a Data Processing Agreement
D. standard contractual clauses
Explanation: there is no point to Binding Corporate Rules, as it concerns an external service. Binding Corporate Rules are meant for international organizations with international data traffic. B, C, and D are required.

A high school is taking its annual school photo. Most students are excited, but some are insecure about their appearance and only join because they think they have no choice, as well as due to peer pressure from their classmates. For students younger than 16 years of age, the school has asked the parents for permission. All parents have consented to a school photo being taken of their child, and explicitly allowed the photo to be taken and sold to all classmates of their child.

To make use of the social media hype, the school uploads all school photos to its social media page, so all students can tag each other and share the photo on their own social media page as they like. The option to tag is widely used, but most notably misused. One girl is tagged as "Fatty McGee", and a boy wearing a Yarmulke is tagged in an anti-Semitic fashion. The next day, these tags in the photos are used to tease these two particular students.

The school quickly receives requests to remove the tags, but is unable to, because the tags were not placed by the school. As a last resort, the school removes the photos completely, but alas, the photos and their negative tags have spread.

16. What can be said about the school uploading the photos to social media?
A. the uploading to social media is not compatible with the original purpose (correct)
B. the school has obtained consent for the photo, and cannot be held responsible for the results of uploading the photo
C. the social media site is fully responsible for what happened with the photo
D. the school is in full compliance
Explanation: the parents consented to the photo being taken and spread to all children. The consent does not cover social media, which results in the spreading beyond the children of the school. A is the correct answer.

17. The Yarmulke can be linked to religion. What can be said about the student?

A. the photo of the child wearing the Yarmulke contains sensitive personal data, as it exposes the child's religion (correct)

B. only the anti-Semitic tags are sensitive personal data, as they explicitly reveal the child's religion

C. unless someone's religion is explicitly mentioned, it should not be considered to be sensitive personal data

D. the Yarmulke does not constitute sensitive personal data, but the size of the girl tagged as "Fatty McGee" is sensitive personal data as it indicates health issues

Explanation: a Yarmulke quite likely indicates the boy's religion, adding the information of the boy's religion to the photo. Although it is manifestly made public and the processing restriction does not apply, A is the correct answer.

18. If wearing the Yarmulke were indeed considered as resulting in a photo containing sensitive personal data, what can be said about the processing restrictions?

A. the school photo has to be deleted, since it contains sensitive personal data

B. the child wearing the Yarmulke needs to be blurred to make him unidentifiable

C. the sensitive personal data has been manifestly made public, so there is no processing restriction (correct)

D. educational institutions are exempt from the processing restrictions

Explanation: C is the correct answer, as the boy wears the Yarmulke in public, making it public that he likely follows a certain religion.

19. Which of the following is not a risk when uploading the photo to social media?
A. the school loses control and is unaware which processing takes place after uploading
B. the school is sued for processing sensitive personal data (correct)
C. the school can be held accountable for the damages caused by uploading the photo
D. after deleting the photo, the social media website still processes the photo further
Explanation: B is the least risky, as the sensitive personal data have been manifestly made public, and therefore the restrictions do not apply. A, C, and D are bigger risks, although C may be a bit farfetched.

20. Which of the following can be said about the girl who is made fun of for her weight?
A. weight constitutes sensitive personal data and is not allowed to be processed
B. consent has been obtained, so the uploading is fine even if it is sensitive personal data
C. the girl is younger than 16, so the processing restriction does not apply
D. whether this constitutes sensitive personal data is still unclear, and case law is needed (correct)
Explanation: D is the correct answer, as weight may or may not reveal something about someone's health. B is wrong because the consent was not for uploading the photo to social media.

A well-known hospital, where many celebrities go for their medical treatment and plastic surgery, has been involved in a scandal. After a politician came in, one of the doctors in charge of her treatment was robbed on his way home. Among other things, the folder with hardcopy files he kept in his briefcase was stolen. The hardcopy files contained the notes that he has taken during the treatment of his patients, and the analyses of their illness or treatment.

Upon realizing what he stole, the thief sold the information to a gossip magazine, which published the embarrassing treatment the politician was in the hospital for. The entire country was in shock, and the politician resigned. She lost so much face that she stayed away from the public eye entirely, having to miss the sizeable salary she enjoyed as a politician.

Bringing files home is not explicitly forbidden by the hospital's policies. As a matter of fact, the doctors are not trained in the safe handling of patient files at all. In addition, the entry in the data processing inventory is vague about what exactly is done with the files. You, as an employee of the national Data Protection Authority, have been asked to investigate the situation.

21. What is most likely the first thing you will check after finding out there is no explicit policy in place that covers taking files home?
A. whether the hospital has the required Data Protection Officer
B. whether the required Data Protection Impact Assessment has been performed (correct)
C. whether the hospital has had similar incidents in the past
D. whether the doctor's laptop has the required level of security
Explanation: given the large amount of sensitive data and the other risk factors (such as vulnerable data subjects), a Data Protection Impact Assessment is likely required. Therefore, this is where you look, to learn whether the risk assessment has taken place to determine the appropriate level of protection.

22. If the hospital has an annual profit of one billion Euros, what is the maximum fine it can receive?
A. 20 million Euros
B. 10 million Euros
C. 2 million Euros
D. 40 million Euros (correct)
Explanation: D is correct. 20 million or 4% of global annual turnover, whichever is higher. 40 million is higher.

23. Which of the following is likely not a reason for the hospital to perform a Data Protection Impact Assessment?
A. automated decision-making (correct)
B. monitoring of people
C. data of weak data subjects
D. large amounts of data
Explanation: it is unlikely that automated decision-making is happening for processes where other risk factors are present, hence A is the correct answer.

24. Given that the details were published by the gossip magazine, which of the following is likely true?
A. it constitutes a data breach, but since it already leaked, the data subject does not need to be informed
B. as long as the hospital does not confirm the leak, there is no way of knowing whether the file is accurate, and it is not considered personal data
C. since the breach only concerns one person, the breach does not need to be reported
D. the data subjects need to be informed by the hospital (correct)
Explanation: when a data breach occurs, and something is likely to have consequences for the data subjects involved, you inform them. In this case the politician's medical data were leaked, and informing her might allow her to take precautions. D is the correct answer.

25. During your investigation you are confronted with the information that all other national hospitals have the same level of protection. What does this likely mean for your case?

A. the current state of technology has to be taken into account, so the hospital is free from blame

B. if the Data Protection Impact Assessment mentions benchmarking with other hospitals, it has done sufficient effort

C. this means your scope is now expanded to all other national hospitals

D. nothing (correct)

Explanation: it does not matter that everyone is wrong, you are there to investigate that specific hospital. There may be further investigations, but it does not affect this one. D is the correct answer.

A large chemical company called *GP Oil* frequently looks for talented staff. To attract this talented staff, GP Oil has an elaborate recruitment and hiring process in place with a flashy website where potential recruits are encouraged to apply for vacant positions. An external firm has set up the entire website's structure, including the flow of documents.

The recruitment process consists of sending a motivation letter, filling out a CV online, several interviews, and a personality test. This ensures only the most suitable and highly qualified candidates are hired, and no employees with undesirable personality traits succeed in the recruitment process. GP Oil sees this as needed to prevent hiring unproductive workers, which are then difficult to get rid of given the local labor laws in some countries.

Not only is the recruitment website great for the help with filling vacancies, it also functions as a place to spark interest. To make everyone feel welcome, vacancies are frequently posted for non-existing posts, in order to give people hope. Nobody is hired, but it does provide a large number of interesting CVs, as well as a collection of test results that can be used to create a blacklist of employees not to hire. For example, candidates for which the result of the personality test shows they are emotionally unstable are automatically ignored during future applications.

26. CVs are automatically scanned for key words and phrases. What is most likely true in this case?
A. this automatic checking is not allowed
B. the privacy notice should mention automatic decision-making (correct)
C. candidates are entitled to a non-automated way of checking their CV
D. a CV is considered sensitive personal data, meaning consent is required
Explanation: B is most likely correct, as automated decision-making needs to be mentioned when collecting personal data. It is implied here, that elimination (a decision) takes place based on key words.

27. What is the main issue with the fake vacancies?
A. when the privacy notice states that the position is non-existent, nobody will apply
B. consent is needed to use the CV for other purposes
C. there is no lawful processing criterion for this processing (correct)
D. there are no issues
Explanation: collecting personal data like this cannot be done under the legitimate interest criterion, as they are collected after lying. Also, consent is out of the question, as explicit consent would require the vacancy being false to be mentioned to the data subject before consenting. The usual criterion, performance of a contract, is also not applicable as the vacancy is fake and it thus is not part of a pre-contractual phase. C is the correct answer.

28. When a candidate gets suspicious and requests a copy of his personal data, which of the following is likely true?
A. the fact that the person applied to a fake vacancy can be incriminating, so the company does not have to release that the person applied for that position
B. (at least) all information he sent to the company needs to be provided (correct)
C. until the application process is over, no data need to be provided
D. as the lawful processing criterion *performance of contract* is used, no data need to be provided
Explanation: all information provided by the data subject is the least the company has to send. There is likely more. B is the correct answer. A, C, and D are nonsense.

29. The personality test goes in depth and exposes a lot about the applicant. Which of the following is most likely the smallest risk?
A. when data subjects request access, the full details of the personality test need to be provided (correct)
B. the personality test could reveal sensitive personal information
C. the personality test is excessive for the purpose
D. consent is required for the personality test, which cannot be given freely
Explanation: answer A is not really a risk, B, C, and D are risks. A is the correct answer. D is interesting, because possibly consent cannot be given freely if it is a condition for completing the application process.

30. For the CVs that the Human Resource personnel find interesting to store or distribute, which is the most likely practical concern?
A. getting consent to keep the CVs
B. providing a privacy notice when filing an application
C. copies of the CVs spreading uncontrolled through the company (correct)
D. deleting applicant data from the system
Explanation: practically, personal data spread all over the place. That is why it is important to limit access to begin with. C is the correct answer. A, B, and D are not really concerns, as they are easy to do.

A video gaming company has sold many copies of a particular video game, which has an option where you can play online with your friends or random strangers. It is massively successful, and millions of people play it on a daily basis, resulting in a large number of recorded gaming sessions appearing on social media.

One negative consequence of its popularity is that video game has been pirated a lot, which is what the company anticipated. In order to make up for losses in sales revenue, it has been decided to gather data through analyzing the cookies on the player's device. This is done by the game software scanning the folders on the user's device where cookies and browsing history are usually stored.

In order to be able to create a profile of the users, the company creates a database of unique device properties with the list of websites that user has visited. The information gathered here is very useful for predicting a user's buying habits and there are a lot of interested marketing companies that pay a high price for the information the video game company provides.

The side-business turns out to be so lucrative that the video game company creates an entire department to experiment with the best ways to collect data and create information to sell. All kinds of tracking technologies are tested on the users of the video game, even an analysis tool that can see whether a user has a certain cognitive condition based on the way he/she plays the video game, or whether the user is employed based on the amount of time the video game is played.

31. What can be said about the data collection?
A. as long as the software is downloaded illegally, the practice is fine
B. secret data collection is not allowed in this case (correct)
C. browsing history is not personal data, so it is allowed
D. making up for lost profits weighs heavy on the legitimate interest balance
Explanation: data cannot be collected secretly in this instance, and information should have been provided in a privacy notice. A, C, and D are just not true.

32. The company revises its privacy policy, and users now have to consent to this data collection before being able to play the game. What is the most likely reason the consent will be invalid?
A. the consent will not be clear
B. the consent will not be freely given (correct)
C. the consent will not be specific
D. the consent will not be reversible
Explanation: if you have bought something, and it is useless if you do not consent to sharing data, then you paid money for nothing. Therefore, customers likely do not feel free to refrain from consenting, hence consent is not freely given. B is the correct answer.

33. After the financial losses have become significant, the company bans users that have pirated the game. It does so based on the serial number on the user's device. What can be said about this practice?
A. the serial number of a device can be considered personal data if it can be traced back to someone (correct)
B. the serial number of a device only says something about a device and is not personal data
C. no information about what is being linked to a serial number is necessary in a privacy notice
D. the company can refuse users access to the information linked to the serial number of their device
Explanation: anything that says something about a natural person is personal data, also the serial number of a device to which the account of a person is linked. A is the correct answer. It should be clear from the context that option B is not the case.

34. When the company collects data about users in order to sell those data, what is the company?
A. a processor if it has not yet found a buyer
B. a controller if it has not yet found a buyer (correct)
C. always a processor
D. neither a processor not a controller until a buyer is found
Explanation: it is a controller, as it did not collect the data on someone's request and determined its own means and purposes. B is the correct answer. Whether it has found a buyer is likely not relevant, but during the exam you may find correct answers with irrelevant additions to throw you off.

35. Whenever a user achieves a high score, the user can choose to upload it to the company's server so that it is visible for other users. What is required in this case?

A. consent

B. legitimate interest

C. a privacy notice (correct)

D. a Data Processing Agreement

Explanation: users need to, at the very least, be informed about the consequences are for their personal data when they take a certain action. C is the correct answer.

A logistics company operating from a massive warehouse has recently been the victim of theft. Some of the more valuable shipments have been stolen from the warehouse. These shipments contained popular video game consoles and flat screen TVs, and are now being kept in the high value area, for which access is granted only to foremen.

As another measure to prevent future theft of shipments, the logistics company plans to install CCTV cameras in the warehouse. This way, the warehouse can be monitored 24 hours a day, so that regardless of when the theft occurs, it will be recorded on video. A nice High Definition CCTV camera is being used, as this provides for proper identification in case of theft.

Before installing the CCTV cameras, the works council is asked for advice. The works council is always involved when changes happen that affect the work or business, and it is even legally required to give advice on any changes. As expected, the works council rejects the idea and its advice is negative.

As the works council only gives non-binding advice, the company goes ahead and installs the CCTV cameras. Every area of the warehouse is now being monitored 24 hours a day, including during office hours when workers are present in the warehouse.

36. What is most likely the criticism of the works council?
A. CCTV is too expensive for the amount stolen, and other ways are recommended
B. the works council says that under no circumstances can CCTV be justifiable at the place where workers load the truck
C. the logistics company first needs to exhaust other means before resorting to CCTV (correct)
D. a pay increase is needed to compensate for the decrease in privacy
Explanation: if it has not been investigated whether less intrusive means can be used, the works council will likely label CCTV as too extreme. C is the correct answer, since the option that leads to the least processing of personal data always has the preference (as long as the goal is achieved).

37. What would be the most acceptable motivation for installing CCTV?
A. it is too costly to track shipments in the warehouse and identify where the shipments were taken
B. GPS tracking of packages at risk is too privacy invasive
C. it has been established that someone sneaked into the warehouse during office hours to steal the shipments (correct)
D. in addition to detecting theft, it allows for monitoring compliance with other company rules
Explanation: the situation mentioned in option C most likely indicates that the warehouse requires monitoring during shifts as well.

38. It has been established that the theft likely occurred at night when no workers were (supposed to be) present in the warehouse. Which of the following most appropriately describes the situation?
A. CCTV can be installed, buy only activated outside of office hours (correct)
B. CCTV is allowed to be active the entire day, as it is still possible workers have stolen shipments as well
C. the employer can force workers to consent to CCTV monitoring
D. if the works council agrees, CCTV is allowed
Explanation: since there is no need to collect personal data through CCTV during office hours, the CCTV should only be switched on after office hours. A is the correct answer.

39. When installing CCTV, which of the following is required?
A. a clearly visible sign with information regarding the CCTV (correct)
B. a privacy notice posted on the employee board in the cafeteria, visible for everyone
C. a privacy notice by e-mail, which every employee needs to consent to
D. a consent form
Explanation: data subjects need to be aware that their personal data are being collected, and need to know how to get more information. A is the correct answer. B and C would miss non-employees, so is not sufficient. D is impossible, as the workers would feel pressured, resulting in consent not being given freely.

40. What is an important consideration when receiving data access requests?

A. the effort to provide someone access to CCTV is disproportionate

B. passport and one other form of ID are needed, to be provided in person

C. balance the interests of the person requesting access with the other person(s) visible (correct)

D. CCTV images can be deleted when a person requests access

Explanation: when receiving an access request you cannot just provide personal data of others in addition to that data request. A balancing of interests needs to take place. C is the correct answer.

A small paper company called *Dunder M* has hired you as a Data Protection officer. Their main activity is to sell paper to other businesses, not to individuals. As such, they do not target individual consumers but have a sales team that contacts the potential customers by calling the phone number that is listed on the potential customer's website. Usually this leads to a receptionist who transfers the call to the right person.

Recently it has been the victim of a cyber attack. At first, it suspected the refrigerator company next door to have pulled a digital prank, but soon it found out the cyber attack was serious. All computers are locked by ransomware, and a message is displayed that the data has been copied to a secure location and it will get the data back if a ransom fee is paid.

Although the ransom fee will mean that there will be no budget for the annual bonus, the CEO of Dunder M is desperate and considers paying the perpetrators, by transferring Bitcoin. After consulting the corporate head office, it is decided to pay the ransom. The data, however, are never returned, and all employees are unable to work without their data.

41. As a Data Protection Officer, what is your first priority?
A. reporting the incident to the Data Protection Authority
B. informing the CEO
C. finding out what data have leaked (correct)
D. paying the ransom fee
Explanation: first it has to be established what has been leaked, because if no personal data have been leaked it is not something a Data Protection Officer needs to be concerned about (although security and data protection go hand in hand). C is the correct answer.

42. In which case would the incident likely not be considered a data breach?
A. if no backup is available
B. if the hard drives are only encrypted (correct)
C. if the data are transmitted to the secure location in encrypted form
D. if the information contains only business contacts

Explanation: if the ransomware made the data unusable by encrypting the hard drives, but the perpetrators have not actually accessed the data, it is not considered a data breach (if you have a backup). B is the correct answer.

43. Which of the following statements is most correct?
A. the Data Protection Officer has 72 hours to report the data breach if it meets the conditions
B. the Chief Information Security Officer determines whether it is a breach that has to be reported
C. all data breaches need to be reported if personal data are involved
D. the organization has 72 hours to report the data breach if it meets the conditions (correct)
Explanation: it is the organization that is responsible for reporting, within 72 hours after noticing the incident, so D is correct.

44. What if no personal data were accessed by the cyber attackers, but all data were lost?
A. if no backup exists, it is still a data breach (correct)
B. the incident does not have to be reported
C. the incident is not considered a data breach
D. data subjects do not need to be informed
Explanation: personal data that being lost but not accessed unauthorized is still a data breach, as this can still have consequences for the data subjects (for example, they will have to supply the data again). A is the correct answer.

45. Which of the following would most likely result in Dunder M informing the data subjects?
A. if all phone numbers of the business contacts were leaked
B. if financial data of customers were leaked
C. data subject do not need to be informed, since Dunder M only deals with businesses
D. if employee files were leaked (correct)
Explanation: employee files likely contain data that can be misused, such as social security numbers, thus requiring the company to inform the data subjects. D is the correct answer.

A marketing company named *Trend Analysis Digital* offers several services. First, it offers to send out mass e-mails to a list of recipients provided by the customer. Second, it offers a survey service, where it contacts persons based on a list provided by the customer or the description of the category of persons described by the customer. Third, it offers a web analysis service where browsing habits of individuals are monitored. All of these services are available to any organization, and are tailored to the customer's needs.

Trend Analysis Digital's first customer in 2019 is an online retailer that sells sneakers. The retailer would like to know who its customers are and what its customers think of the services it provides. Trend Analysis Digital designs a package of services for the retailer, which includes a survey for his customers and an analysis of what type of people the retailer's customers are.

The data that are collected are not stored under any name, but are only given a unique ID. Attached to this ID are the data, such as browsing habits/history, preferences, submitted survey results, etc. If available, an e-mail address is also stored under the profile, in case Trend Analysis Digital would like to contact that person because he/she fits a profile for which it has have a survey.

46. If an e-mail is sent out with a survey after a product is ordered from the retailer's website, which of the following is needed?
A. an opt-out only
B. consent and a discount
C. a web beacon
D. parental consent for minors (correct)
Explanation: parental consent is required for many digital processing involving underaged data subjects, so D is correct. A web beacon is never needed (in the context of data protection), consent coupled with a discount is likely not freely given and an opt-out for surveys is likely not sufficient.

47. If Trend Analysis Digital uses a social media web beacon to link the visitor to a social media profile to see which type of people buy from the website, which of the following is most likely used?
A. legitimate interest
B. opt-out
C. consent (correct)
D. performance of a contract
Explanation: a web beacon, when used this way, practically results in transferring personal data to a third party, where in this instance consent is likely the only valid lawful processing criterion, meaning C is the correct answer.

48. For the survey, the online retailer offers a 5 Euro discount on the next purchase if the customer's data can be used. Which of the following is most true?
A. by providing a 5 Euro discount, the legitimate interest lawful processing criterion can be applicable
B. by providing a 5 Euro discount, the legal obligation lawful processing criterion can be applicable
C. the consent is not valid if the use of non-anonymous survey data is a condition for the 5 Euro discount (correct)
D. once consent has been provided for the survey data, the consent is irreversible
Explanation: consent needs to be given freely. If the 5 Euro discount is only given if consent is provided, then the data subject may feel pressured to consent as he/she otherwise does not receive the discount. So C is the correct answer.

49. For every marketing e-mail sent out, there are tracking technologies that record what the recipient does with the content. Which of the following is most likely true?

A. if the tracking technologies do not allow for anonymous data collection, these tracking technologies are not allowed to be used

B. unless the data are collected without being able to identify the person, consent is the only valid lawful processing criterion (correct)

C. when a data subject requests erasure of all his/her data, it is not sufficient to irreversibly remove his/her name and other identifiers from the data set

D. if the data subjects did not opt-out, the tracking technologies are allowed to be used

Explanation: B is the correct answer, as there is no likely interest that would justify the invasion of privacy of seeing who opens which e-mail at what time, unless consent is given. If the person cannot be identified, it is likely not personal data so no consent is needed.

50. Since the web beacon is technically loaded from a third party, what can be said about the requirement for a privacy notice?

A. the third party is fully responsible for providing a privacy notice

B. even though it is a third-party web beacon, what happens still needs to be mentioned in the privacy notice (correct)

C. the website is not responsible for providing a privacy notice for the web beacon

D. although responsible for providing a privacy notice, it is practically impossible to do so, hence there is an exemption

Explanation: if when visiting your website, external tracking technologies gather data, you are still (at least in part) responsible for it. Therefore, it needs to be mentioned in a privacy notice, answer B is the correct answer.

Turbulent Assessments, a company that gathers and analyzes public data on any person, has become quite popular. The service started two years ago, right after several terrorists turned out to have infiltrated a large multinational to use its recourses for their cause.

The way Turbulent Assessments works, is that its customers submit the name of the person they want screened, after which its software scrapes the internet for that person's personal data. The software then creates a predictive psychiatric evaluation, allowing the customer access into the prediction of that person's behavior. This can be used for a variety of purposes, such as screening job applicants to see whether he/she fits the department or the screening of compatibility of potential spouses.

Being incredibly successful, Turbulent Assessments has received a lot media attention. This media attention has also led to scrutiny by the Data Protection Authority. No violation has been established yet, but Turbulent Assessments has received a request for information, and it appears to be quite time consuming to respond to the request in a timely fashion. Turbulent Assessments has responded to the Data Protection Authority that the request for information may be somewhat unrealistic and asked whether it can get an extension of the deadline.

51. In this scenario, which statement is not applicable to Turbulent Assessments?
A. if Turbulent Assessments performs its analysis to screen potential job applicants, it requires a Data Processing Agreement
B. Turbulent Assessments requires a lawful processing criterion to process the public data
C. any individual using the services of Turbulent assessments is outside of the scope of the General Data Protection Regulation
D. all data used by Turbulent Assessments are public, so they are outside of the scope of the General Data Protection Regulation (correct)

Explanation: public data are within the scope of the General Data Protection Regulation, meaning organizations cannot just use them without respecting the data subjects' rights. In addition, any analysis results are not public data. D is the correct answer.

52. If Turbulent Assessments stores its data scrapings (so not the analysis results) using a cloud service, which of the following is applicable?
A. no extra safeguards are required, as it only concerns public data
B. no lawful processing criterion is needed, as it concerns public data and thus in line with the original processing purpose
C. a Data Processing Agreement is required (correct)
D. data breaches have no consequences for public data
Explanation: even though the personal data are public, a processing agreement is still required. C is the correct answer.

53. Which of the following is most likely true regarding Turbulent assessment's obligations to comply with any request from the Data Protection Authority?
A. since the analyzed data are public, all Turbulent Assessments' activities are acceptable
B. Turbulent Assessments has to cooperate (correct)
C. no new personal data are generated during Turbulent Assessments' work, so there will be no contact with the Data Protection Authority
D. Turbulent Assessments only needs to cooperate if a data breach occurs
Explanation: of course it needs to cooperate. B is the correct answer.

54. When Jack receives a rejection from a company where he applied for a job, and it motivates the rejection with a negative public assessment, which of the following is most likely not true?
A. the company was supposed to inform Jack that the assessment was part of the procedure
B. consent would have been invalid
C. the employer is the Data Processor (correct)
D. the employer is the controller
Explanation: the employer is a customer, and not a processor. Likely the employer is a controller, as it uses the data it bought in the way it wants. C is the correct answer. Turbulent Assessments may be a data processor, depending on the specifics, which are missing in this case. During the exam you will encounter questions with context missing, and you will have to ask yourself if the context is relevant for the question (often it actually is not) or whether you can derive certain things from the facts provided in the question.

55. Which of the following statements is most likely true regarding Turbulent Assessments?
A. depending on the context, they can be either Data Controller or Data Processor (correct)
B. Turbulent Assessments is always responsible for providing the data subject a privacy notice
C. when Turbulent Assessments moves to the US it will immediately fall out of the General Data Protection Regulation's scope
D. Turbulent Assessments is exempt from the access request obligation, as it concerns public data so the data subject has full access already
Explanation: if customers request Turbulent Assessments to perform its analysis, then Turbulent Assessments is likely a processor. If Turbulent Assessments performs the analyses and then sells them to customers (so the targets were picked before) it is likely a controller. A is the correct answer.

Brendon, an ex-employee of a Dutch University, is curious about the personal data his previous employer still processes. It has been three years since he left, and he starts with consulting the privacy notice posted on the University's website. The privacy notice has changed quite a bit since Brendon worked at the University, so it takes him a while to go through all the information.

According to the most recent privacy notice, the way to receive a copy of your personal data is by submitting a request to the University's Data Protection Officer. Brendon sends an e-mail to the University's Data Protection Officer to request a copy of his personal data. The Data Protection Officer at the University receives the request and, somewhat disgruntled, starts the process of gathering the personal data of Brendon.

All relevant persons at the University are informed of the request. One department however, informs the Data Protection Officer that it has personal data of Brendon, but will not be handing over a copy of the data. The department claims it does not have to, which the Data Protection Officer is then asked to assess. After assessing the situation, the Data Protection Officer concludes that the University is indeed not required to hand over these data to Brendon.

56. When receiving Brendon's request for access to his personal data, what is most likely the University's first reaction?
A. ask Brendon for a reasonable fee for the access to his data
B. ask Brendon to identify himself (correct)
C. inform Brendon his request is too large, and that the University wishes to extend the period of responding
D. tell Brendon that he had the chance to access his data at the time he was employed at the University, meaning the University is not required to comply with his request
Explanation: identification is the first step. If a data subject refuses to provide identification (to the situation-dependent required extent), then the University does not have to provide the data, so doing anything until identification could be wasted effort. B is the correct answer.

57. Regarding the time to react to Brendon's access request, which of the following is correct?
A. the University can immediately inform Brendon that his request will take longer than the 30 days
B. the University has 20 days to respond to Brendon's request
C. the University has 30 days to respond to Brendon's request (correct)
D. none of the answers are correct
Explanation: 30 days is the period to respond. C is the correct answer.

58. The department that processes Brendon's personal data and refuses to provide Brendon with access is most likely which of the following?
A. a science department (correct)
B. the legal department
C. human resources
D. medical services
Explanation: countries have the freedom to exempt personal data used for scientific purposes from the right to access, so A is likely the correct answer. B could also be the case, but A is more likely. Use the *most likely* approach at the exam if you are doubting between two answers.

59. The University responds to Brendon with the remark that it does still have Brendon's data in its system, but that it is not processing the data, and hence denies Brendon access to his data. Which of the following statement is correct?
A. storing is not processing, hence Brendon can be denied access
B. storing is also processing, hence not a reason to deny Brendon access (correct)
C. Brian consented to the storage of his data, which result in a waiving of access rights
D. Brendon has full access rights to the stored data
Explanation: B is correct. Storing data is also processing. D is not necessarily true for all data.

60. After a lot of hassle Brendon gains access to part of the data the University stores on him. He finds out part of it is embarrassing and tells the University to delete it. Which of the following is true in this case?

A. the right to be forgotten is an absolute right, so the University must comply

B. the right to be forgotten outweighs any lawful processing criterion the University can have, so the University needs to comply

C. the University does not need to comply, since Brendon is no longer a University employee

D. if the University has a legal reason to keep the data on Brendon, it may keep the data (correct)

Explanation: there can be legal reasons (such as fiscal duties) to process certain personal data, in which case you have no right to be forgotten. D is the correct answer.

You have just fallen ill, in the sense that you have an embarrassing issue for which you do not wish to consult a medical practitioner. Instead, you turn to the internet and order the medication you think you need, from the *Pharmacy of Canada*. The online pharmacy seems reliable, as you can pay in Euro and select your local language.

When you receive the medication you decide not to use it, after you balance out the risks of self-prescribed medication with the medical condition that may or may not be real. You throw the suspicious looking package with medication in the trash and forget about the whole situation. And, a few days later, your condition disappears, comforting you in having taken the right decision regarding the use of the medication.

Then, after some months, you receive a phone call, asking if you are interested in cheap erectile dysfunction pills. This is completely unrelated to the medication you ordered in the past. On top of that the phone call is unwanted and you had forgotten all about the order you placed. You ask the caller to never call you again, because if you need something you will call. From the caller's response it is unclear whether the caller will comply with your request.

61. Which if the following is likely true regarding the website?
A. the Canadian website falls outside of the scope of the General Data Protection Regulation
B. the website is based outside the European Union, and the data need to be handled compliant with the General Data Protection Regulation (correct)
C. the General Data Protection Regulation does not apply, because the website does not contain information on natural persons from the European Union
D. only the e-privacy directive is relevant in this case
Explanation: the website was in your local language and you could pay in Euro, so it is obviously targeted at data subjects in the EU. Therefore, the data need to be handled compliant with the General Data Protection Regulation, and B is the correct answer.

62. In order to contact you by phone, which of the following was likely needed?
A. consent was required
B. nothing was required, as you are customer
C. freely given consent was required
D. the opportunity to have opted out (correct)
Explanation: it could be allowed to contact someone if the personal data were collected in the context of a sale, but an option to opt-out needs to have been provided (as well as with each communication that follows). D is the correct answer.

63. Which of the following can be said about the type of data the website handles?
A. buying certain medication can be seen as sensitive personal data (correct)
B. the website handles orders, not personal data
C. medication is always considered sensitive personal data
D. there is no certainty the medication is actually used, so there are no sensitive personal data involved
Explanation: although common pain killers may not reveal much, if you buy medication for any specific disease it can be quite revealing and seen as sensitive personal data. A is the correct answer.

64. All of a sudden you see an advertisement on social media, with the medication you ordered from the online pharmacy. Which of the following could most likely be true?
A. the website has processed your data without a valid lawful processing criterion (correct)
B. social media sites sniff your device for invoices
C. your key strokes were logged by the social media site
D. you consented to being shown advertisement based on cookies placed by other websites
Explanation: B, C, and D are unlikely. A is likely true, as web beacons are tricky and revealing, especially in the context of sensitive personal data, in which case consent would have been needed. A is likely the correct answer.

65. If the company turns out the be from within the European Union, which of the following is likely true?

A. no intercontinental laws apply

B. an opt-out at the time of sale was needed (correct)

C. no Data Protection Impact Assessment is needed

D. Binding Corporate Rules are necessary

Explanation: A, C, and D are nonsense. B is the correct answer, similar to the question before.

You just started a new job, as Data Protection Officer of a video streaming service. Ever since the video streaming service started, you have been a big fan. You really feel like it is a company that contributes to the flourishing of society by allowing users to share content with everyone who is interested.

The first day on the job you start meeting your colleagues, but most importantly you inspect the personal data processing inventory. Your idea of a prudent first day is to know the processes so you can ask whoever you speak to about the processes he or she is responsible for. Going through the personal data processing inventory, you see a lot of red flags. Many processes seem to be secretive and unnecessary for the services the customers buy.

One example is secretly keeping track of the viewing history, and placing the person in a category. These data are then used to recommend shows to that user. Where you first thought that these recommendations were a friendly service to the user, you now find out they are based on what the producing company of a TV show is paying the streaming service to recommend to, for example, a single white heterosexual male.

66. What is likely the biggest reason the identified red flag will lead to uncovering a non-compliant practice?
A. the labeling is not needed to provide the service the customers pay for
B. the categories attached to a user contain sensitive personal information (correct)
C. there is no non-compliance, the legitimate interest criterion is applicable
D. it is forbidden to process sensitive personal information
Explanation: in this case, consent is required for processing sensitive personal information, which the sexual preference category above is. B is the correct answer, although the others also have some risk. D is phrased tricky, as it is true but not answering the question. Note that, to mislead, this question talks about personal *information* instead of personal *data*.

67. What is not a task of the Data Protection Officer?
A. inform the CEO
B. instruct management to reprimand the employee responsible (correct)
C. educate the organization
D. give negative advice regarding the situation
Explanation: option B is outside of what can reasonably be expected from a Data Protection Officer.

68. If a data subject requests access to his/her data, which of the following is not true?
A. the data not provided by the data subject, do not need to be provided (correct)
B. Binding Corporate Rules in place will not prevent access to data stored outside of the European Union
C. the CEO has final say in whether the data subject is provided access
D. the data subject does not need to show a valid form of ID
Explanation: even if a data subject did not provide the data him/herself, they are still part of the data in an access request (unless certain exceptions apply).

69. Which of the following would you expect to find for the process of placing customers in categories?
A. separate servers for category data
B. a Data Protection Impact Assessment (correct)
C. a category is not personal data
D. CEO approval
Explanation: given the sensitive nature of the categories and the large number of users, a Data Protection Impact Assessment would be a good idea. B is the correct answer. D may be true, but does not relate to data protection.

70. Which of the following is likely true for the customers outside of the European Union?

A. unless Binding Corporate Rules are in place, a Data Processing Agreement needs to be in place

B. HIPAA preempts the General Data Protection Regulation

C. unless citizens outside the European Union are specifically targeted, they do not fall within the scope of the General Data Protection Regulation

D. they require the same protection as citizens from the European Union (correct)

Explanation: D is correct, the video streaming service is located in the European Union and needs to protect the data for all data subjects the same way regardless of origin (not taking into account any stricter laws in other countries).

On a nice and sunny day, you decide to visit an amusement park with your friends for a day of fun and excitements, riding roller coasters and other rides. The most spectacular ride, a giant roller coaster called *The Goliath*, is the most popular of all. You and your friends spend half of the day riding it.

At end of the day, on your way home, your friends discuss the day. During the discussion a remark is made about how it looked like your glasses were almost flying off on the last picture. With an awkward smile on your face, you ask "who took a picture?". Your friends react surprised to you not having seen the photos displayed when exiting the ride. You actually did not recognize those as being taken that day, and your eyes were closed at the moments the pictures were taken.

Although you are not happy with being photographed without permission, you do understand that it is part of the business model of the amusement park and that it is quite common to take photos during a roller coaster ride. You would have liked to have had the opportunity to see the photo and be able to purchase it. When you arrive home you decide to send an e-mail to the amusement park about it, requesting a copy of the photo.

71. How should you have found out about the photo?
A. the photo is being deleted, so informing the person afterward is sufficient
B. you should have been provided with the option to consent to the photo, or not go on the roller coaster
C. you should have been informed right after entering the amusement park
D. before taking the photo, you should have been informed (correct)
Explanation: organizations need to provide the information on the processing before collecting the data, so at the very minimum it needs to be pointed out that a photo was about to be taken (not counting exceptions, like journalism). D is the correct answer, although in practice very few amusement parks (if any) are complaint.

72. When you get home it does not sit well with you that the amusement park has taken your photo without asking for your permission. You send an access request. What is likely true for the access request?

A. the company needs to send you all your personal data, including the photo if they still have it (correct)

B. the photo also contains other people, and therefore can be withheld during an access request

C. since the amusement park took the photo to sell, it can charge a fee for it

D. the amusement park can send you your data without the photo, if it informs you the photo is visible in the amusement park itself

Explanation: an access request should contain all the personal data the amusement park has of you, unless it would violate the rights of others. In this case, other people in the picture can be made unrecognizable or cut out completely, so there is no reason not to provide the photo. A case could even be made that the photo has to be provided in the highest quality possible, as the sharper an image, the more revealing. A is the correct answer.

73. If the amusement park wishes to use the photo for its website, which of the following is likely true?

A. the photo falls under the exemption for journalism and can be freely used

B. a fee needs to be paid for the use of the photo

C. the amusement park needs to obtain consent, even if it does not know who the persons in the photo are (correct)

D. the amusement park can rely on the legitimate interest lawful processing criterion

Explanation: obviously consent is required, as it was a photo taken for commercial purposes. Not knowing who someone is does not mean you do not have to obtain consent. C is the correct answer.

74. After sending an access request, you find out the amusement park keeps the photo in a backup in case a visitor wants to order another copy. You request the deletion of your photo, but the amusement park refuses. Which of the following is likely not true?
A. the amusement park needs to crop you out of the photo
B. the amusement park can rely on the legitimate interest lawful processing criterion, as it would be too much work to crop the photo (correct)
C. the amusement park should not have kept the photo
D. the amusement park has not obtained valid consent
Explanation: B is nonsense, so the correct answer. The amusement park does not have the right to keep your personal data like this against your will, regardless of the other people in the photo wanting to order more copies. A photo is also cropped without much effort.

75. After your access request, you receive a weekly newsletter, as it turns out the amusement park has placed the e-mail address you used for the access request on a mailing list. Which of the following is likely true?
A. until you opt-out, it is allowed to keep you on the mailing list
B. the amusement park needs to provide an opt-out with their newsletter (correct)
C. you have visited the park and did not opt-out, so the amusement park has compliantly placed you on the mailing list
D. an e-mail address is not personal data, since anyone can choose any e-mail address
Explanation: the amusement park needs to provide an opt-out, B is the correct answer. It also needed to ask for consent, as it obtained your e-mail from your access request, but that was not one of the answers.

An energy company deals with frequent phone communication. Although the company has a website, most people cannot figure out the solution quickly enough or cannot spare the effort. For that reason, the energy company employs a large team of phone operators that are standing by 24 hours a day to assist customers with any questions or issues.

Dealing with customers on the phone is quite complicated and stressful. Many phone operators make mistakes, resulting in angry customers. The angry customers, in return, cause a large amount of psychological stress, resulting in staff with a burnout and other mental health issues.

For that reason, the energy company has created an elaborate training program. All phone calls are recorded, analyzed and used for training if something can be learned from it. These lessons learned are then used to train new and current phone operators, allowing for continuous improvement.

The company plays an automatic recording at the beginning of any phone call that mentions "this phone call can be recorded for training purposes". This brings the recording to the customer's attention and allows the customer to hang up the phone if he or she does not want to be recorded, hence fulfilling the obligation to inform customers about the processing of their data.

76. What can be said about the message about recording the phone call?
A. if the recording is indeed used for training, the information is not sufficient
B. the information is sufficient, since the recording starts after the message
C. data subjects provide consent by continuing the conversation after the recording
D. the information is not sufficient (correct)
Explanation: there are several things missing in the information provided in the phone call, which are required by article 13 of the General Data Protection Regulation, hence it is not sufficient. D is the correct answer.

77. One of the data subjects is quite annoyed by the recording, and objects to it. Which of the following is most likely true?
A. the recording cannot be stopped and the objection is not valid
B. if the energy company has a legal duty record verbal contracts, the objection will not stand (correct)
C. if the Binding Corporate Rules state that phone calls are recorded, the objection will be invalid
D. the privacy notice on the energy company's website explains the process in detail, hence the data subject cannot object
Explanation: you cannot object when the company is legally required to processes your data that way, so B is the correct answer. If, for example, it relies on legitimate interest you would be able to object. D may seem true, but this assumes that the person read the privacy notice before calling (which may not be the case), and still does not necessarily allow for the practice.

78. If a data subject requests access, does the energy company have to provide the voice recording of the customer?
A. no, as the recording also contains the phone operator's voice
B. no, as sending the recording is disproportionate
C. yes, access needs to be provided (correct)
D. the energy company will only be obliged to provide the recording if the customer provides a storage medium for the recording
Explanation: C is correct. Perhaps the voice of the operator needs to be altered or removed, but the recording of your voice is your personal data and you should receive access.

79. What can be said about the recorded message if the phone operators are located outside of the European Union?
A. the privacy notice on the website will need to be updated so that calling customers know their data are recorded outside of the European Union
B. safeguards need to be in place (correct)
C. customers need to provide additional consent
D. the General Data Protection Regulation no longer applies
Explanation: A and C may be correct, but not necessarily (a privacy notice on a website is not really practical when you are on a phone call with an urgent question, and providing consent is unlikely to be freely if you have an urgent question). B may be vague, but the best option in this case.

80. The energy company uses smart meters, that automatically create an energy profile of the customer. Which is likely true?
A. the processing beyond the used energy goes beyond the purpose for which it was collected (correct)
B. the smart meters are illegal
C. the customer does not have to consent to receiving an energy profile report
D. no processing beyond the original scope is allowed
Explanation: B and D are a little extreme. C is a grey area. A does not say much, but is correct, as the meters should measure energy and not create profiles linked to a person.

You are working for an internationally operating social media website, targeting users all over the globe. Millions of users make use of the website on a daily basis, and large amounts of personal data are stored all over the world on cloud services and private servers.

To access their data, data subjects only have to log on and click the "download my data" button. All the data they uploaded to the website is then packaged in a compressed folder and through a link it can be copied to their local device. The whole process goes automatically, and takes only a few hours.

Identification is done through logging on, and to prevent anyone from taking over the account when the user is not looking or is automatically logged on, the link to the collection of data is sent only to the e-mail address used to create the social media account.

Then, one day, the Data Protection Officer receives a data access request by telephone. The user says she has lost her password, user name and e-mail account used for her social media account, but would still like to get a copy of her data. All options for recovering the password the conventional way are impossible, and it appears a decision needs to be made regarding the access request.

81. What is likely true for this access request?
A. as she uploaded the data herself, she already has access to the data, and a copy does not have to be provided
B. the personal data, including the website script, need to be provided
C. the social media website needs to also provide the revenue it makes of its users
D. a copy of the personal data has to be provided (correct)
Explanation: A is wrong. B is too much. C is too much. D is correct.

82. What can be said about identification before providing any personal data?
A. no identification is required, as she uploaded the data herself
B. only a personal visit showing a valid passport or national ID is sufficient
C. a video call could be sufficient (correct)
D. providing a new e-mail address, so the account can be reset, is sufficient
Explanation: a video call could establish the identity, especially if it can be compared to the content of the social media page and a valid ID. A and D are scary if put into practice. B is an option, but not the only option, hence incorrect.

83. Which of the following is likely not true about data subject identification?
A. not requiring identification leaves the risk of giving the wrong person access to someone's data
B. sending the password and user name by post is a reliable way of providing only the right person with access (correct)
C. using a known e-mail address or phone number for verification is a reliable way for the social media site to verify
D. the social media website needs the highest possible level of certainty in the identification
Explanation: sending it to a postal address provided by the person calling still does not provide assurance that the person who is on the phone is the owner of the social media profile. B is the correct answer.

84. The social media site does not only keep data that the users provided themselves. Which of the following is likely true?
A. there is no possible lawful processing criterion for this practice
B. since the social media site is used free of charge, the practice is justified
C. if the users did not provide the data themselves, they are not personal data
D. all personal data need to be provided (correct)
Explanation: all personal data need to be provided, including the personal data generated by the social media sites (such as categories a user is placed in). D is correct.

85. The social media site allows other websites to use the social media site's web beacon so it can store which websites are visited by the users of the social media site. What can be said about this practice?

A. it does not result in personal data, since a visited website is not a natural person

B. as long as the collected data are not used for advertisement, it falls outside of the scope of the e-privacy directive

C. it is deceiving and difficult to implement legally (correct)

D. although personal data, the social media site can use *legitimate interest* to not have to notify users of the data collection

Explanation: implementing it in a legal way would likely require consent, which would be provided to the website that contained the web beacon, which data subjects would need to be able to withdraw, which would create a whole messy process. C is the most correct answer.

Traffic in the city is getting worse and worse. Commuters are frustrated and tourists prefer a less crowded city. Accidents are also occurring more and more often, especially given the number of international workers who are used to a different way of driving.

Then, one day, you see a large number of scoot vehicles spread throughout the city. These vehicles are placed there by a company called *EZ Scoot*, in an effort to reduce car traffic in the city. The vehicles are small and easy to use, allowing the young and hip people, as well as the old and rusty people, to go to work or go to their favorite avocado restaurant.

In order to use the scoot vehicles you have to install an application on your phone and scan the code of the scoot vehicle. The vehicle is then unlocked, and your account will be charged for the time you use it. Of course, to prevent theft, all scoot vehicles emit a GPS signal which EZ Scoot can access whenever it wants. If a vehicle has not been used for a certain period of time, someone is sent to the location where it has been left to check on the vehicle. Most of the times it has been damaged, but other times it has been taken into someone's home.

86. What can be said about the GPS signal?
A. the GPS data are personal data
B. the GPS data are not personal data
C. the GPS data could be personal data (correct)
D. no information is collected
Explanation: if a GPS signal goes from one location to another, this could mean the person's home and work. Where someone works or lives is personal data. C is the correct answer.

87. Which further processing would most likely not fit the purpose?
A. selling data for the most visited places to a marketing company
B. optimizing traffic based on the places most travelled through
C. storing the GPS data linked to the users (correct)
D. sending the coordinates of a stolen scoot vehicle located in a residence to the police

Explanation: storing personal data (GPS data linked to users) is unnecessary. C is the correct answer.

88. What can be done to ensure the GPS signal is not personal data?
A. unlink beginning and end location from profiles
B. restrict the area in which GPS signals are tracked (correct)
C. only store usernames, not actual names
D. do not store any type of name
Explanation: if no homes or work locations are in the area it is unlikely to be considered personal data (provided that it is not linked to a user). B is the correct answer. Option A implies it still links users to GPS data. C ignores that usernames can also be/contain personal data. D has similar issues as C.

89. If a scoot device is stolen, the data are sent to the police. What can be said about this practice?
A. an unacceptable practice
B. the GPS data are not personal data
C. the police will not take any action, as they are not allowed to process the personal data
D. likely an acceptable practice (correct)
Explanation: B and C are not likely. A and D could be correct, but A is a strong answer in a grey area, so D is the correct answer since it has the word 'likely' in it.

90. You use a scoot vehicle every now and then, and request EZ scoot to sent you a copy of your personal data. Which of the following is likely true?
A. GPS data are not personal data, so no data need to be provided
B. only financial transaction data need to be provided
C. you only have the right to be forgotten, not the right to access
D. whatever EZ scoot stores about you, has to be provided (correct)
Explanation: as you should know by now, D is the correct answer (given some exceptions that likely do not apply here).

Made in the USA
Columbia, SC
10 December 2021

50918175R00057